Hertfordshire

Nick Corble

COUNTRYSIDE BOOKS
NEWBURY BERKSHIRE

First published 2007

COUNTRYSIDE BOOKS
3 Catherine Road
Newbury, Berkshire

To view our complete range of books,
please visit us at
www.countrysidebooks.co.uk

ISBN 978 1 84674 018 3

Maps by Gelder Design & Mapping

Photographs by the author
Cover picture of the Grand Union Canal
supplied by Derek Forss

Designed by Peter Davies, Nautilus Design
Produced through MRM Associates Ltd, Reading
Printed by Borcombe Printers plc, Romsey

Contents

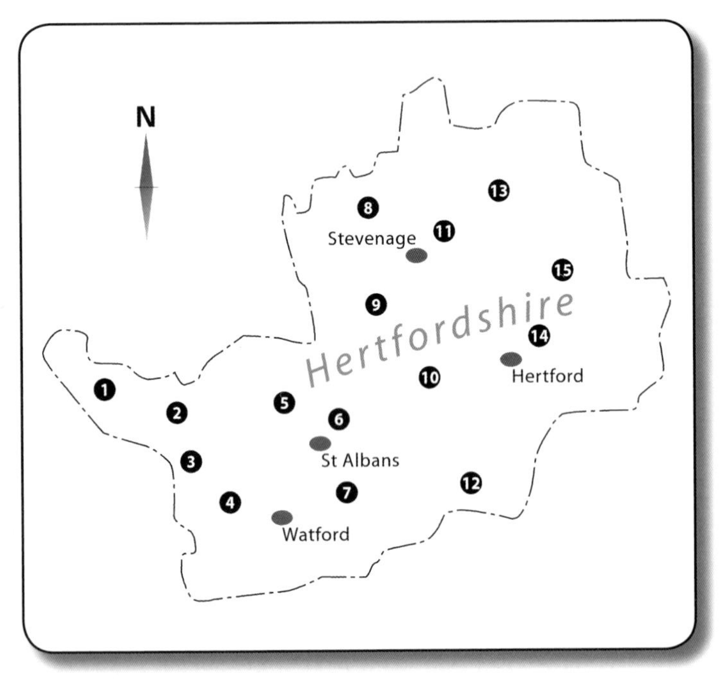

Area map showing location of the walks

Introduction

I was born and brought up in Hertfordshire and thought I knew 'my' county pretty well. It came as a surprise therefore, when writing this book, to find out how wrong I was. A pleasant surprise, mind you, as plotting and plodding my way round the countryside I discovered such a wealth of landscape and stories that I feel I have at last earned my spurs and can properly regard myself as a 'Hertfordshire Hayabout', the traditional nickname for people from the county.

This name is a corruption of *haystack* and refers to the cornfields which define the local countryside and traditionally helped to feed the capital to the south. Indeed, another of Hertfordshire's defining characteristics is that it is a land beyond the metropolis, the first port of call outside London, and this becomes evident in these walks.

Each walk has been chosen to explore these rural roots and without exception they rely on public footpaths and bridleways to guide the reader round the county. Where possible, other thoroughfares have also been used, such as riverside walks, abandoned railways or canal towpaths. A recurring feature is one of openness, showing just how uncrowded this part of the world is. In a matter of moments the walker is alone, with just the wide skies and the sights and sounds of the countryside for company.

In the walks I have tried to direct the reader to otherwise unknown pubs, hidden jewels in Hertfordshire's crown, the tracking down of which has been my special pleasure! Thus, this book is perfect for keeping in the glove compartment of your car for that moment when you feel like sampling somewhere new.

Don't set out unprepared, however. Use of an Ordnance Survey map, ideally from the Explorer series, is strongly recommended, as is appropriate footwear. The walks in this book are not long — they range from 2½ to 5½ miles but there's nothing worse than being stuck in mud halfway round! And for the same reason, consult the weather forecast and take appropriate clothing.

An idea is given in the introduction to each walk of the type of refreshment you might expect at each pub, from gastro to pub grub at its best. Be prepared for serendipity, though, as owners and chefs change, as do opening times. The phone number of each recommended pub is provided so that you can check, and to make life easier, suitable parking spots and directions are also given.

Finally, each walk has a suggestion of somewhere else you might wish to visit while you are in an unfamiliar area, and I have tried to provide a range of attractions to allow you to achieve a deeper understanding of what makes, or has helped to make, that area's character.

I cannot finish without thanking those who provided encouragement and company, not least my son Edward. Being a teenager he'll deny it, but I suspect he shared some of my enjoyment of fresh discovery, as indeed I hope you, the reader, will too. Happy walking!

Publisher's Note

We hope that you obtain considerable enjoyment from this book; great care has been taken in its preparation. However, changes of landlord and actual closures are sadly not uncommon. Likewise, although at the time of publication all routes followed public rights of way or permitted paths, diversion orders can be made and permissions withdrawn.

We cannot, of course, be held responsible for such diversion orders and any inaccuracies in the text which result from these or any other changes to the routes nor any damage which might result from walkers trespassing on private property. We are anxious though that all details covering the walks and pubs are kept up to date and would therefore welcome information from readers which would be relevant to future editions.

The simple sketch maps that accompany the walks in this book are based on notes made by the author whilst checking out the routes on the ground. However, for the benefit of a proper map, we do recommend that you purchase the relevant Ordnance Survey sheet covering your walk. The Ordnance Survey maps are widely available, especially through booksellers and local newsagents.

1 Aldbury

The Greyhound

Tucked away on the edge of the Ashridge estate, Aldbury is a well kept secret. Its church houses an effigy whose feet rest on a so-called 'wild man', while the large duckpond and preserved stocks provide a focal point. Peeping over the trees near the start of the walk is the Bridgewater monument, dedicated to the man known as the 'Father of Inland Waterways', who also happened to own nearby Ashridge.

The walk takes in the monument, but first there's a steep climb into the woods surrounding it, although there is a National Trust shop and café at the top where you can rest. The route then progresses through Aldbury Common, which is carpeted with bluebells in spring and foxgloves in summer. Some of the trees are over 300 years old and, where they have fallen, they are often covered in wild honeysuckle. There are meadows and

Distance 3¾ miles

OS Explorer 181 Chiltern Hills North, GR 965125

Terrain One very steep hill near the start but after that mainly woodland and field-side walking along bridleways

Starting point The Greyhound pub; park outside the pub or in the village.

How to get there *Aldbury lies two miles west of Tring, along Station Road. Follow signs for the station and continue for a mile.*

views along the way and a choice of pubs in the village – so why not start in one and finish in the other?

THE PUB

The ivy-clad **Greyhound**, just beyond the magnificent pond in the heart of the village, consists of a warren of rooms, including a public bar and a restaurant with a choice of seating areas. One of these is an elegant conservatory where the art on the walls is for sale. Outside in summer there's bench seating at the front, with tree stumps to rest your pint. There's a good choice of beers, including Badgers, Sussex Best and Tanglefoot. The lunch menu includes dishes such as smoked haddock, free range pork sausages and mash, and toasted paninis, with more exotic fare in the evenings.

Open Monday to Saturday 11 am to 11 pm; Sunday noon to 10.30 pm.
Food is served Monday to Saturday from noon to 2.30 pm and from 6.30 pm to 9.30 pm; Sunday from noon to 4 pm.
☎ *01442 851228*

1 From the pub, turn right and right again and walk up a lane towards a playing field with a kissing gate in the corner. Ignore this, heading right down **Percy Crow Lane** and passing a paddock on your left. The path narrows a little before coming out on a sports field. Bear right and go through the entrance and then right again. Cross the road, where you will see a waymarker on your left sending you up the hill into the woods via a stile. The route now heads along the side of a meadow, which can be resplendent with butterflies in summer.

2 In the corner of the meadow the path enters the first of this walk's woods and begins to head sharply uphill, with a number

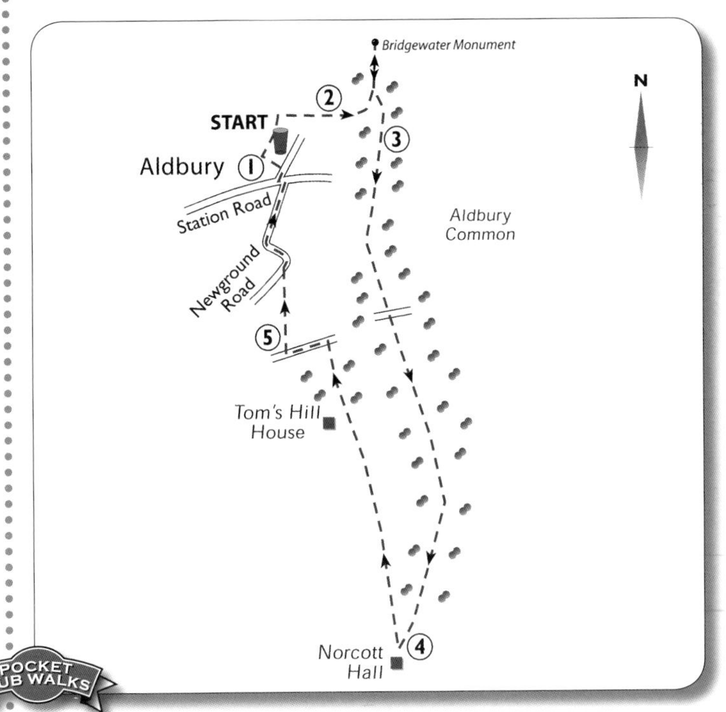

POCKET PUB WALKS

of badger sets along the way. Just as you may be thinking you've had enough climbing you come out onto a track, where you turn left, to continue uphill, but much more gently, and come out onto a large open space with the **Bridgewater Monument** and its turquoise top in front of you. After your sightseeing, go back down the track but take the first spur to the left, down a track marked 'no horses', where the path becomes flat.

3 At a fork, keep left and follow the path as it winds through the trees and over a track near a remnant of **Gryme's Dell**, a variant of Grim's Ditch. This continuous Saxon earthwork was spread across the Chilterns, but only fragments now remain. On reaching a road, cross it and follow the marker for the Ashridge Estate Boundary Trail, which is also part of the **Icknield Way**, ignoring possible diversions on either side. After a short while the path comes out alongside an area of open land to the right. Take the next left-hand fork (marked with the sign of an axe), and after passing through more trees emerge onto open land. Turn right and keep to the edge to reach a dog leg and then continue straight ahead into more woods.

The Bridgewater Monument was erected in 1832 in honour of the 3rd Duke of Bridgewater.

4 On reaching a junction by more open land, bear right to emerge from the Ashridge estate onto a private road, where you head right, following an impressive brick wall belonging to **Norcott Hall**. Continue past some cottages, aiming slightly right at the fork and cutting down the side of a meadow, with a view

of **Tom's Hill House**. On reaching a minor road, head left and, after 100 yards, pick up the path on your right by a grass triangle. This leads back into some woods, where there is a spectacular display of foxgloves in summer, and heads steadily downhill and bears right.

The village stocks at Aldbury.

5 At a junction of paths head straight on where the route cuts diagonally across a large meadow with a stile hidden in the middle. This brings you downhill to a metal gate, a stile, and a road, where you turn right. Follow the road to the left and then to the right by the **Valiant Trooper pub** and you will come out by a post office, village stocks and a large duckpond, which together announce that you are back at your starting point.

Places of interest nearby

Tring is well worth a visit, both for its **Memorial Gardens** and the **Walter Rothschild Zoological Museum**. The latter includes preserved specimens of countless animals, fish, and insects and even boasts a dodo! Now part of the Natural History Museum, this is open daily from 10 am to 5 pm (2 pm to 5 pm on Sunday; ☎ 0207 942 6171). The gardens were originally the lily ponds of the local manor and an entire hamlet was demolished to create them. They now commemorate the fallen of the two world wars and include a magnificent Wellingtonia tree.

2 Berkhamsted

The Crystal Palace

Welcome to Berkhamsted and Greeneland, so called because of the town's connections with Graham Greene, whose father was once headmaster of the local school, which the great author also attended. Berkhamsted Common, featured in this walk, is the spot where, as a young man, Graham Greene is known to have played his infamous game of Russian roulette, and the walk's featured pub, the Crystal Palace, was used in his last book, *The Captain and the Enemy*. In his novel, however, Greene called it The Swiss Cottage, which was the name of the timber yard that used to sit opposite and formed an integral part of an area known as the Port of Berkhamsted. These days this site is marked by a totem pole, which was carved by a member of the Kwakintl tribe and is a memento of many years trading between the yard and Canada.

This walk is steeped in history and fittingly starts by passing the ruins of Berkhamsted Castle, which is significant for being the spot where William the Conqueror was finally handed the English crown in 1066. After a short stretch along roads, the route heads into the countryside and the woods that ring Berkhamsted Common. Following a leg-stretching stroll through fern-lined paths it heads south across fields with an excellent view towards the town, and ends with some easy canal-side walking.

THE PUB

Perched on the side of the Grand Union Canal, the **Crystal Palace** was once a favourite haunt of canal boatmen using the so-called 'Port of Berkhamsted'. It gets its name from the fact that the building was designed by Joseph Paxton, like its namesake at the Great Exhibition. Today the pub retains an unpretentious air, although the sawdust that until recently covered the floor is now gone. There are separate public and lounge bars, and the latter is lined with timber wainscoting and functional furniture. There is some waterside seating outside and plenty of canal memorabilia on the walls. The pub specializes in roast dinners, served all afternoon on Sundays, and at other

Distance 4¾ miles

OS Explorer 181 Chiltern Hills North, GR 996078

Terrain A couple of steep hills, but these are not long; otherwise mainly a combination of fieldside, woodland and towpath walking

Starting point The Crystal Palace pub; park outside the pub

How to get there *Berkhamsted sits on the A4251 between Hemel Hempstead and Tring. Follow signs for the Castle.*

times offers a range of substantial Chinese and Thai dishes served with a choice of chips, fried rice, or noodles, which are enough to satisfy anyone's stomach.

Open Monday to Saturday from 11 am to 11 pm; Sunday noon to 10.30 pm. Food is served Monday to Saturday from noon to 3 pm and from 5 pm to 11.30 pm; Sunday from 12.30 pm to 5 pm (roast only) and from 6 pm to 10.30 pm.
☎ 01442 862998

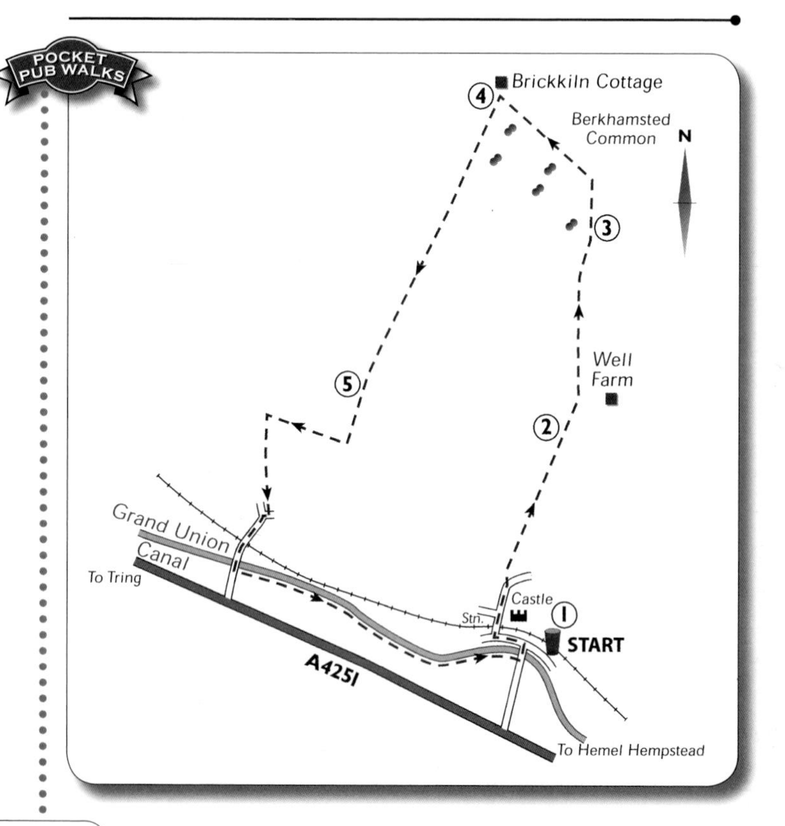

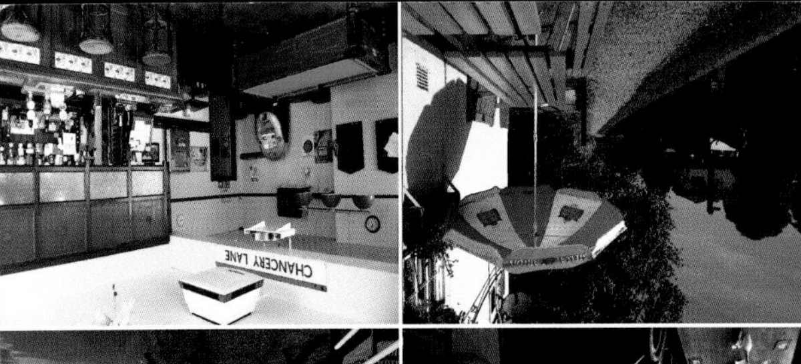

The Crystal Palace

Station Road, Berkhamsted, Hertfordshire HP4 2EZ

Tel: 01442 862998

Pete & Tina welcome you to

The Crystal Palace

Sunday Carvery 12:30 - 5:00pm

Chinese Food Monday - Saturday

Canalside Seating

Disabled Facilities

Live Music Thursday & Saturday

Real Ales

Open All Day 7 Days a Week

Credit Cards Accepted

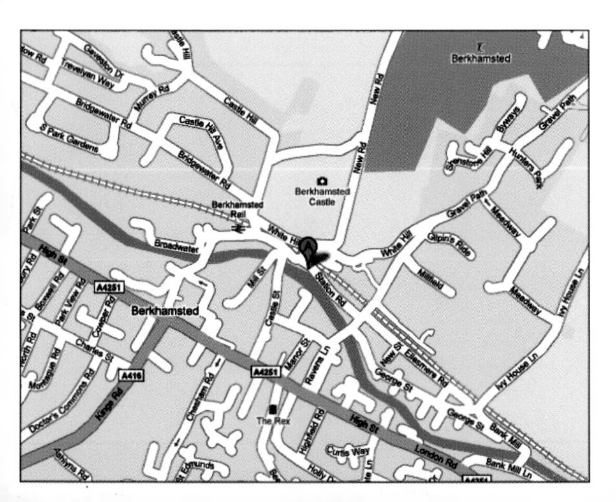

Berkhamsted Castle where William the Conqueror was handed the crown in 1066.

1 Turn left out of the pub on the railway side and follow the road towards the station, turning right into Brownlow Road and passing the clearly visible ruins of **Berkhamsted Castle** on your right (see below). Cross Bridgewater Road, heading uphill, and maintain your direction where the road bends to the right; pick up the footpath at the top, signed to Berkhamsted Common. This in fact passes up the side of a road leading to the playing fields of Berkhamsted School.

2 The path soon turns into a grassy track and enters open countryside, with **Well Farm** ahead acting as a marker. On reaching the farm the path diverts slightly to the left but otherwise remains easy to follow as it heads towards some woods. It can become muddy underfoot here; so be careful, although there is some compensation in the rich variety of fruits in the ancient hedgerows to your left.

3 Go into the woods via a stile, bringing you onto **Berkhamsted Common**. Pass through some trees until you get to a narrow bridleway, distinguished by a profusion of ferns, where you need

to turn left. At a fork in the path, take the right-hand option, clearly marked by blue bridleway arrows, and follow the path until you reach another junction of paths near an isolated cottage, **Brickkiln Cottage**, on your right.

4 Here you need to go downhill to the left. On reaching the edge of the wood, bear right and cross over a stile. The path now emerges onto an open field and heads quite steeply downhill into a small valley, with an equally challenging climb up the other side. After another stile maintain your direction at a junction of paths, again heading downhill and then uphill and passing an incongruously placed memorial seat. Here there is a splendid view of Berkhamsted and beyond.

5 The path now descends to a stile in the corner of a field, with a school playing field ahead. Cross the stile and head right until you reach another junction of paths, where you turn left. Pass in front of the entrance to the school and walk along a concrete path behind some houses, emerging eventually onto a residential road. Cross this and go down to the railway line, crossing the tracks via the bridge. At the next bridge go over the canal and turn left onto the towpath. The final mile or so takes you beside the **Grand Union Canal** and a series of locks through the flatlands which would have once constituted the **Port of Berkhamsted** and back to your starting point.

Places of interest nearby

Although it may not be so obvious today, **Berkhamsted Castle** has a long and often surprising history. It is open to visitors all year round and is well worth a visit.
☎ *01442 871737*

In addition, there is an excellent **Graham Greene Trail** and a **Heritage Walk**, leaflets for which can be obtained from the library and civic office on the High Street.

3 Flaunden

The Bricklayers Arms

Now sensibly sited on a hilltop, Flaunden is in fact much older than it looks — it's just that it has moved. Until two centuries ago it sat a couple of miles further down in the Chess Valley, but its inhabitants got so fed up being flooded that they upped sticks and relocated. This included the church, today's building dating back to just 1837, while its predecessor could trace its origins to the 13th century. Nearby Bulstrode's history goes back even further, with archaeological digs revealing evidence of a Neolithic or Bronze Age long barrow.

These days, both villages are neat local communities. Flaunden has two pubs, the second of which, just outside the main part of the village, is the starting point for this walk. The route follows mainly fieldside boundaries, cutting across the minor roads that link the area together. The going is easy and pleasantly rural, with crops or horses occupying the fields. Bulstrode marks the limit of the walk, which then heads back towards Flaunden, which, if the

Ordnance Survey was more imaginative, would be marked on maps with 'here there be dragons', although only one is visible today!

THE PUB

The Bricklayers Arms, located in the hamlet of Hogpits Bottom, just outside Flaunden, is a 200 year old, award-winning gastro-pub, its exterior walls clad with Virginia Creeper. Inside, the pub is characterized by very low beams and wood. A long narrow bar gives out onto a similarly streamlined garden backing onto a paddock. The kitchen has recently been the recipient of a stockpotful of awards, including Chef of the Year; and this is reflected in the menu. Offerings include such delights as sausages on a chive mash, and steak and kidney pie marinated in Guinness, whilst beers include Greene King IPA, Fuller's London Pride and Morland Old Speckled Hen.

Open from noon to 11 pm daily. Food is served from noon to 3 pm (4 pm on Sundays), and from 6.30 pm every evening.
☎ *01442 833322*

Distance 3¾ miles

OS Explorer 182 St Albans and Hatfield, GR 017014

Terrain Flat, mainly on field paths with some country lanes

Starting point The Bricklayers Arms; use the parking provided, having first sought the landlord's permission.

How to get there *Flaunden lies two miles north-east of Amersham, off the A404. Turn left in Flaunden to reach Hogpits Bottom.*

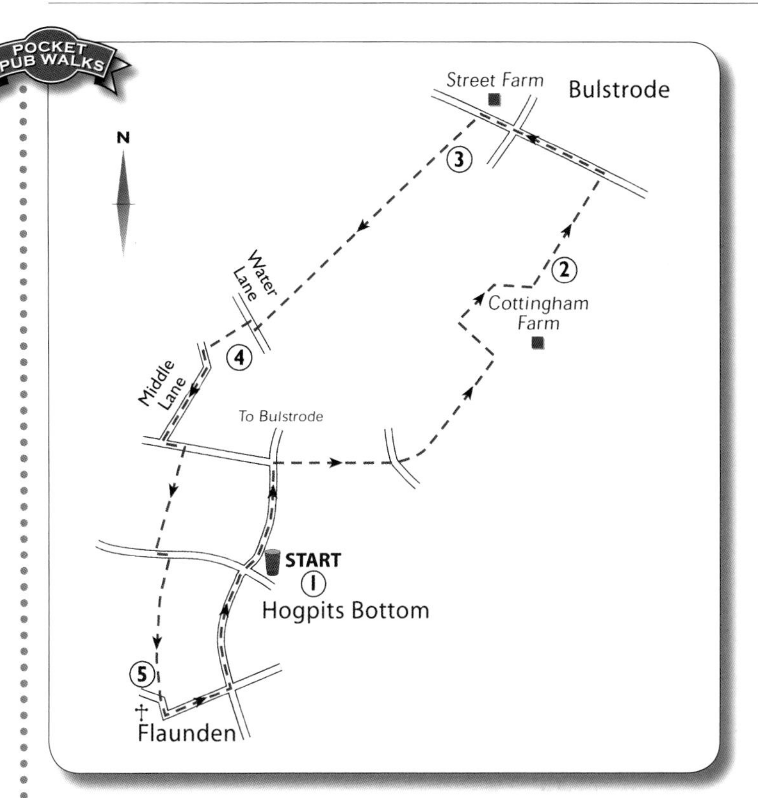

1 Turn right out of the pub and then right again at the crossroads, towards Bovingdon. Just before reaching a turning to the left, take a track on your right, signed Hatton House. Immediately before the house, keep to the path where it forks to the left via a kissing gate; pass a junction with another path on your left and go through another gate. Cross over a narrow road and then keep first to the right-hand and then to the left-hand edge of the following fields. Just before **Cottingham Farm** follow the fingerpost to the left. An elaborate diversion around the farm now follows before you regain your previous direction.

2 The path continues straight ahead, following the right-hand edge of a field and heading into **Bulstrode**. On reaching the road, cross over and head left by a bus stop onto **Chipperfield Road**, passing some cottages. There's a pavement here which takes you past a crossroads. About a hundred yards further on, opposite **Street Farm**, pick up the footpath on the left. Bulstrode is known for its lack of hedges, as 29 were grubbed up to form the single large field you are about to cross.

3 Pass through a kissing gate signed to **Water Lane** and enter the large open field. (First, however, there is some horse grazing followed by yet another kissing gate before you finally cut across the middle of the field.) Aim for the gate at the end of the field where the low hedge meets some trees. The path now passes behind some stabling. On reaching Water Lane, turn right, and

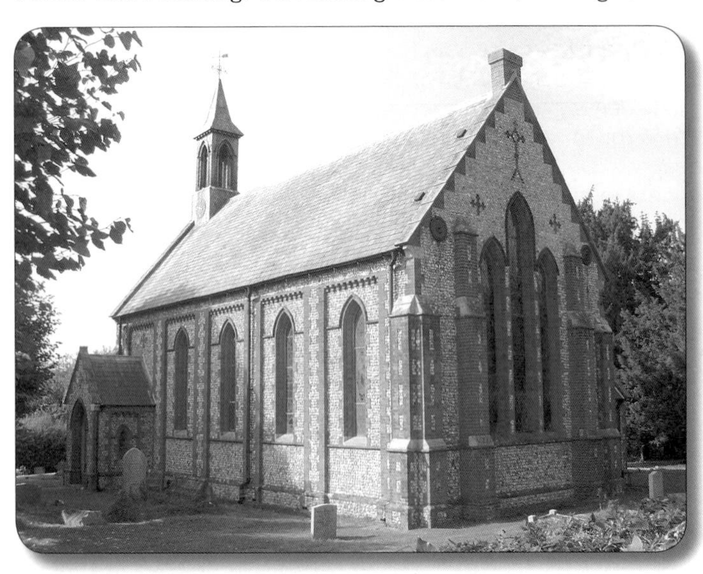

Flaunden's distinctive square flint church

then immediately left down a footpath signed to **Middle Lane**.

A dragon peers over the trees in Flaunden.

4 The route is now channelled down the side of a fence. Turn left into Middle Lane and follow the bend round to the right. At the T-junction turn left. After 30 yards, pick up the path on your right signed to **Flaunden** and follow it down the right-hand edge of a field bounded by a metal fence and past a static caravan site. Turn left at the road and once again pick up the footpath on your right, which has now become a bridleway.

5 The path comes out by **Flaunden church**, which is distinctive with its flint exterior and square aspect. Whilst taking in the church, look behind you at the green dragon's head which can be seen peering over the trees. Turn left at the church and follow the road round, to pass the Green Dragon pub (whence your earlier experience). Follow the road to a crossroads, where you turn left and continue past some cottages and the **Old Chapel** (whose owner has the dubious privilege of having a garden composed largely of gravestones), before returning to the crossroads at your starting point.

Places of interest nearby

If you've got used to open spaces, **Chipperfield Common**, 2 miles east of the pub, is worth a visit. It includes a route that leads to a 400 year old Spanish chestnut tree, some prehistoric burial mounds, a dew pond, and the Apostles' Pond, so named because it is surrounded by a dozen lime trees. These were planted in 1714, and one, which has failed to thrive, is known, perhaps inevitably, as the Judas Tree.

4 Chandlers Cross

The Clarendon Arms

It's hard to believe you're just off the M25 and two miles away from Watford when doing this walk. Chandlers Cross is little more than a hamlet, dominated by its pub and cushioned from 'civilization' by a series of deciduous woods, the most prominent of which is Whippendell Woods. Once part of the nearby Cassiobury estate, the wood is now designated a Site of Special Scientific Interest and harbours a rich variety of flora and fauna.

Distance 5½ miles

OS Explorer 172 Chiltern Hills East, GR 066983

Terrain Can get slippery in the woods during bluebell time; some short sharp hills, but otherwise generally flat along well-defined paths

Starting point Either the pub (using the car park, with the landlord's permission) or the public car park in Whippendell Woods (GR 074977).

How to get there *Chandlers Cross is 2 miles north of Croxley Green, ½ mile south-west of Junction 19 of the M25, and just west of Watford.*

This walk gives an opportunity to explore the woods, and the clearings that were created during the great storm of 1987 and now offer options for picnicking. On leaving Whippendell, the route meets the Grand Union Canal and follows the towpath for a while before entering fresh woodlands, which, like Whippendell, are particularly glorious in late spring when bluebells carpet the floor.

THE PUB Commanding a prominent position between two road junctions, the **Clarendon Arms** has a sweeping L-shaped bar with seating on different levels, the whole area being defined by two stone-faced fireplaces, and half-height wood panelling gives a warm feel to the place. The beers available here include Old Speckled Hen and Wells Bombardier, and the food on offer ranges from a selection of pies (including a quiche of the day) to a tapas board and delicacies such as *pescados fritos* (whitebait with horseradish) and *chorizo con queso* (pan fried spicy sausage with mozzarella cheese). The pub also has a patio outside and a large car park.

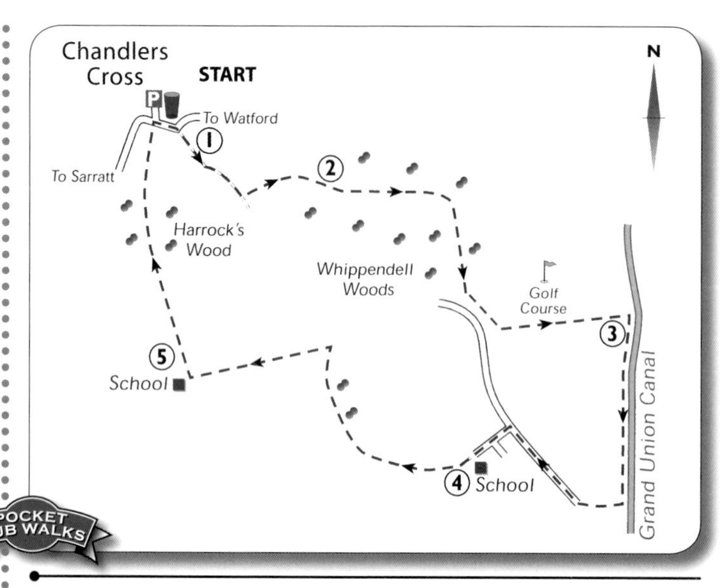

Open Monday to Saturday 11 am to 11 pm; Sunday noon to 11.30 pm. Meals are served from noon to 3 pm and from 6 pm to 9 pm.
☎ *01923 270929*

1 Turn left out of the pub and walk down **Rousebarn Lane** on your right, following signs to **Blackett's Nurseries**; the road soon enters woodland. Just after the entrance to the nurseries, take the footpath on the left, signed to **Watford**, which leads you into **Whippendell Woods**. (An information board on the right notes that this Site of Special Scientific Interest is known particularly for its wide variety of fungi and insect life, including speckled wood, ringlet, and holly blue butterflies. These woods also served as the Naboo Forest in the Star Wars film *The Phantom Menace*.) The track is broad and easy to follow, with occasional clearings offering possibilities for picnics.

2 On reaching a triangular junction of paths, keep to the right and, shortly after, at another junction, in a clearing, take the right-hand path, heading south-west. At the end of this path, near a road, bear left and continue until you reach a fingerpost sending you left and signed to '**Cassiobury Park**, 820 yards'. (All these woods were once part of the Cassiobury estate.) After a slight uphill climb, you encounter a golf club, and the path takes you over a fairway; so look right for flying balls! Pass through another stretch of woodland and then cross another fairway before descending to a bridge over the **Grand Union Canal**, known as Iron Bridge, with a lock to the left. A couple of old lock beams have been positioned as seats by a commemorative plaque celebrating the bicentenary of the canal in 1987.

3 Pick up the towpath heading south (the bridge side of the lock) and follow this down to the next bridge, approximately ½ mile. Turn right here and go uphill, following a sign to **Chandlers Cross**.

The lock and Iron Bridge over the Grand Union Canal.

Descend the hill to come out by some houses, where you head right into **Rousebarn Lane** (the opposite end from where you started). Follow the lane until, at the end of the houses, you reach a road on the left, **Little Green Lane**, which you take, climbing uphill to a school.

4 At this point the lane becomes more of a track, but maintain your direction, going to the back of the school. After 100 yards, pick up the footpath on the right, signed **Sarratt Parish Walk**. This passes through a narrow strip of woodland and then tracks half right across some open land. At the far side, take the path to the left at a junction, keeping the woodland to your left. Where the track ends, also by a school, go through a kissing gate and then turn right, following the sign to **Chandlers Cross**. Note the unusual wood-carving on your left.

5 You soon enter **Harrock's Wood**, an ancient woodland, which is known for its bluebells, as well as the rare coral root bittercress, which is visible in spring. The path follows what is known as **Finches Avenue**, a diverse woodland made up of ash, oak, sycamore, cherry and unusual conifers. The deep indentations you may notice are the remains of excavations for gravel and flint. The path emerges from the woods and brings you out opposite the pub where you started.

Places of interest nearby

Cheslyn Gardens in Nascot Wood Road, Watford, are regarded as the town's best kept secret. The 3½ acres have been designed to provide variety and colour all year round in a range of styles, including formal gardens, a rock pool and woodland, and there is also an aviary. The gardens have the added attraction of being free and open every day except Christmas.
☎ *01923 235946*

5 Redbourn

The Cricketers

Redbourn is a distinct community, with its iconic common dominating the area to the west. Once a coaching stop, the village gained a fresh lease of life when the busy A-road linking St Albans and Dunstable was taken round the village, giving it the opportunity to breathe once again. A long history boasts not only one of the oldest cricket grounds in the country but also an industrial heritage that includes the manufacture of silk, straw plaiting and hat making.

The walk passes evidence of all of these activities, and the picturesque Redbournbury Mill, with two nearby fords, provides its centre point. Passing through fields and beside the River Ver on the way, the route takes in the common and an old railway line, with cows and a variety of wildlife for company.

Distance 4½ miles

OS Explorer 182 St Albans and Hatfield, GR 103118

Terrain Largely flat and easy walking

Starting point By the cricket ground, where there is public parking; the pub car park offers limited spaces

How to get there *The common sits to the west of Redbourn village, which is off the A5183, 3 miles north-west of St Albans.*

THE PUB

The **Cricketers** is located on the east side of the common and, as its name suggests, overlooks the local cricket ground, where the game has been played since 1666. This sets the perfect scene for whiling away a hot summer Sunday afternoon. The pub itself is cosy and popular with locals, and no wonder with a good choice of real ales including London Pride and Fuller's IPA. The menu features the usual pub staples plus a house speciality of savoury pancakes, with fillings ranging from curried prawns to bacon, brie and tomato. There are two bars, and the lounge is guarded by an elegant copper horn by the door, suggesting that this was also once a poplar spot for the hunt to gather.

Open Monday to Saturday from noon to 11 pm; Sunday noon to 10.30 pm. Food is served from noon to 3 pm and from 6 pm to 10 pm every day.
☎ *01582 792410*

1 Walk onto the common and into the avenue of beech trees, where you turn right. Keep to the path as it spurs to the left and into **Lamb Lane**. Pick up the footpath leading to **Shepherds**

Row on the right and follow this round the back of some houses to **Redbourn High Street**. Turn right and pass the shops and numerous pubs, a legacy of the village's past as a coaching stop. Continue to the roundabout, passing under a railway bridge that once carried the **'Nicky' line,** a spur linking Harpenden with Hemel Hempstead and now a recreational path. Cross over at the island and continue straight ahead on the path beside the **St Albans** road.

2 Shortly after passing a milestone, pick up the footpath on the left, signed to **Harpenden Common**. This heads half right through a couple of pastures and then into a large arable field where the path is well marked. On reaching a bank with a Christmas tree plantation in front, bear right, keeping to the edge of the field; the path now leads slightly downhill. On coming to another field, turn right, keeping the hedge on your right.

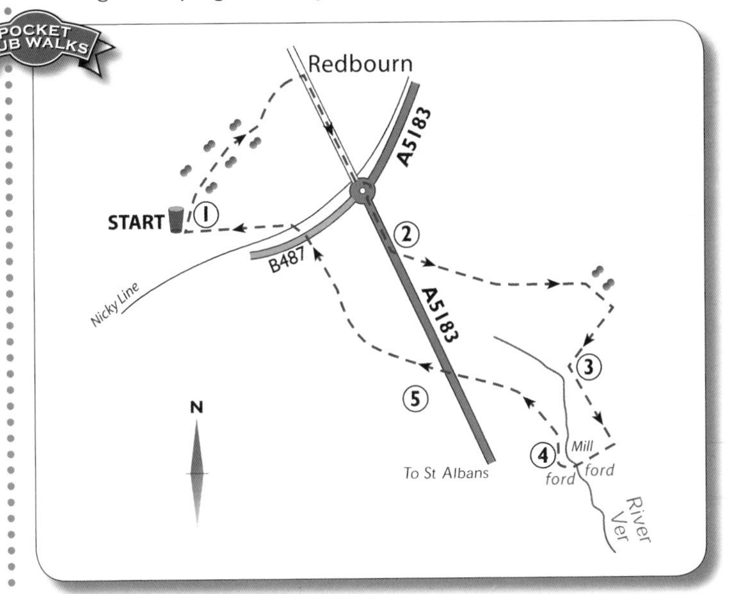

3 Follow the edge of the field to some trees; here you will encounter a well dredged section of the **River Ver** on your right, much favoured by local trout fishermen. From here the river flows into nearby **St Albans**, the Roman name of which, Verulamium, was derived from the river name. The path continues to a ford, the first of two quite deep passages, although on the right there is a wooden footbridge to get you over.

4 Follow the road past the second ford and up to **Redbournbury Mill**. The river here is a favoured spot for reed buntings and skylarks; so keep your eyes and ears open. Pass through the gates of the mill and follow the path through a wooden gate to the left of the buildings. You are now walking on the opposite bank of the **River Ver,** where cattle laze away their days and may show some interest in you. The path soon eases away to the left and eventually comes to the **St Albans** road again.

5 Cross the road and pass through the gate to Millstream, taking the furthest right of the two paths presented to you, alongside a wooden fence. The path emerges into another large arable field, where you turn right. It then widens out into a track and comes to a road, which you cross; then follow the footpath on the other side, once again passing the **Nicky Line**, to some housing. On reaching a residential road, turn left, left again, and then right. Continue on this road, passing some magnificent willows on your left, and return to the common and your starting point.

Places of interest nearby

Redbournbury Mill is worth visiting en route on the walk or coming back to. The present building is the result of a long restoration project. Records show that there was a mill here at the time of Domesday, although the current building dates back to the 15th century.
☎ *01582 792874*

6 Sandridge

The Green Man

Now barely a stop on the road heading out of St Albans, Sandridge was once an important parish, covering much of the northern part of the city. The church at its centre is worth pausing at to admire its memorial lychgate and its flint construction as well as its interior, where there is a list of all the vicars and curates who have served there since Jon Ball at the time of the Black Death in 1349.

The walk is easy and largely flat, and turns at the notorious Nomansland Common. This was the favoured hunting ground of the famous 'Wicked Lady', a female highway robber who is said to have terrorized the neighbourhood. The local pub is named after her, and she was made the subject of a black-and-white film. More recent research has thrown doubt on whether the Wicked Lady ever in fact existed, but somehow it's easy to believe she did when you visit the common yourself.

THE PUB A solid red brick pub conveniently located in the centre of the village, the **Green Man** dates back to the 1880s and these days is a favourite of cyclists and walkers. There is a car park and garden at the back, along with a conservatory for eating in. This is a homely pub with a U-shaped bar and an interesting collection of pictures on the walls, including sets of framed cigar (not cigarette) cards. Abbot Ale and other guest beers are available, and there's an extensive menu, which includes a warm Italian chicken salad and a creamy tomato and herb pasta bake, as well as a very comprehensive mixed grill.

Open Monday to Thursday 11 am to 3 pm and 5.30 pm to 11 pm; Friday and Saturday 11 am to 11 pm; Sunday 11 am to 10.30 pm. Food is served from noon to 2.30 pm, and on Friday and Saturday evenings only from 7 pm to 9.30 pm.
☎ *01727 854845*

Distance 3½ miles

OS Explorer 182 St Albans and Hatfield, GR 171106

Terrain Level, mainly through fields, with a little road walking. Firm paths and bridleways make this a pleasant stroll for all ages, although there is a short stretch of a couple of hundred yards by a busy road.

Starting point The pub, which is unmissable, in the High Street; park in the car park (having obtained the landlord's permission, of course) or alternatively use the layby in Sandridgebury Lane, opposite the church.

How to get there *Sandridge is on the B651, 1½ miles north-east of the centre of St Albans.*

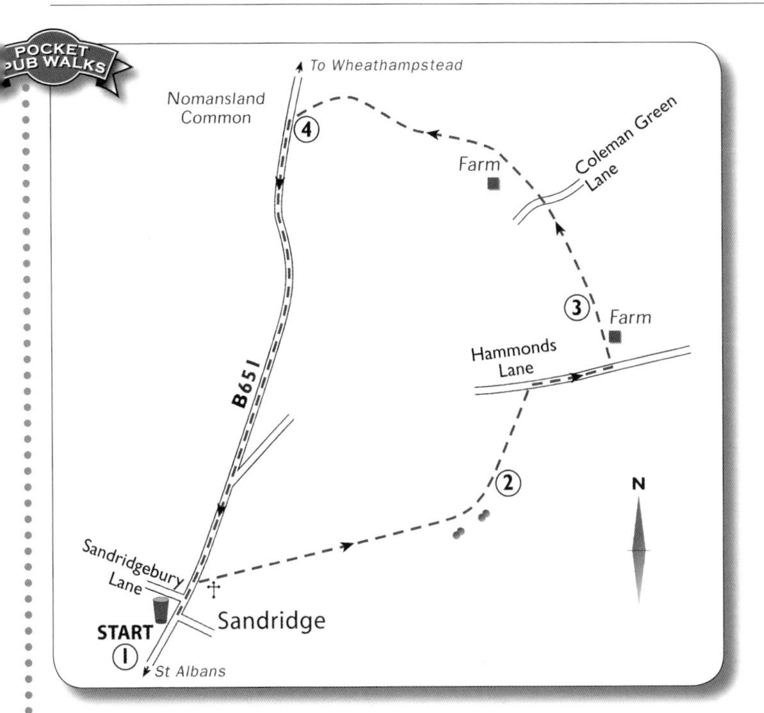

1 Turn left out of the pub, cross over the road, and turn up **Church End** towards **St Leonard's church**, past the **Rose and Crown** pub. Pass through the magnificent lychgate, which is dedicated to the dead from the parish in the two world wars. This is a depressingly long list which is partly accounted for by the fact that until relatively recently the church served a much wider area than the current village. St Leonard, the patron saint of prisoners and pregnant women, is a popular saint in these parts. Pass to the left of the churchyard and go through a gap and on to a footpath, where you turn right.

2 On reaching another road cross straight over and pick up the footpath signed to **Hammonds Lane**. This crosses a large arable field before meeting the side of a small copse of trees, which is well favoured with bluebells in late spring. On emerging from the trees, maintain your direction until you reach a road, **Hammonds Lane**, where you turn right. Go along the road, which is slightly uphill, with high hedges either side of you, until you reach **Hammonds Farm**, taking a moment to admire the spectacular thatched house ahead of you, just off the route, as

The lychgate leading to St Leonard's church, Sandridge.

well as to savour the delicious quiet here and the great views on either side. Turn left into the farm and pass to the left of the house. At a large black-painted barn, head left and pick up the clear bridleway.

3 On reaching a hedge, pass to the right, keeping the brush to your left, and stay with this until you reach a road, which you cross, and then continue along the bridleway. There's another farm to your left, barely visible behind the hedge, although you may just catch a glimpse of a natural pond in its grounds. The path falls away to the right briefly before pulling back to the left onto the outskirts of **Nomansland Common**, which at this point is well wooded. These days the common is shared between two local councils, but it gets its name from a protracted dispute in the 15th century over its ownership between the abbeys of Westminster and St Albans.

4 When you come to another road, go left. Initially at least, this entails walking along the verge and you need to be extra careful, as the brow of the hill can conceal oncoming traffic. Thankfully, the route soon diverts to the right and follows the left-hand edge of a field. Follow this flat and easy path all the way back to the outskirts of Sandridge; here it becomes a metalled pavement leading back to the starting point.

Places of interest nearby

In nearby St Albans is the Roman theatre of **Verulamium**. This was capable of seating 2,000 spectators and uniquely in Britain it had a stage rather than an amphitheatre. There are a number of other Roman antiquities in this corner of St Albans, including the remains of a villa, a hypocaust, and a large expanse of wall. The excellent museum (see walk 7) is well worth visiting.
☎ *01727 835035*

7 Tyttenhanger Green

The Plough

Tyttenhanger Green is a rare spot of rural calm on the outskirts of St Albans, sandwiched between the growing city and the busy road to its south. Its main claim to fame is as the place where owners of Metropolitan cars gather in July every year for one of their rallies. These typical 1950s cars look like something out of the film *Grease* and are well worth seeing if you can.

Given the location of this walk, and the growth of urban encroachment, an Ordnance Survey map is a must, as it's just possible that some of the paths may have been swallowed up since publication of this book, and waymarkers are sometimes lacking. That said, this route gives you an opportunity to sample

Distance 3½ miles

OS Explorer 182 St Albans and Hatfield, GR 184059

Terrain Flat easy walking along field edges and residential paths

Starting point The pub, using the car park with the landlord's permission

How to get there *Tyttenhanger Green is a mile north of the A414, east of the junction with the A1081 and south-east of St Albans.*

what most of the countryside round here, until recently, would have looked like. Much of the route is on well trodden paths alongside fields and farmland with mature hedgerows. Now's the time to enjoy this walk, as the temptation to turn some of these fields into housing estates may prove irresistible before too long!

THE PUB

Just on the edge of Tyttenhanger Green, the **Plough** is the clear highlight of this walk. The very friendly ambiance is reflected in the jokey menu (which threatens that vegetarians will be shot) and may also have something to do with the large selection of beers on offer, ranging from Fuller's London Pride and ESB to half a dozen guest ales. This variety is reflected in the amazing collection of beer bottles from all corners of the globe lining the walls. The menu includes both snacks and specials and offers a selection of fry-ups (cholesterol guaranteed!), all of which are very reasonably priced. The snacks include a variety of croques, including Monsieur and Hawaiienne, and the double-decker Mike's Super Sarny, as well as salads, pies, sandwiches, and jacket potatoes.

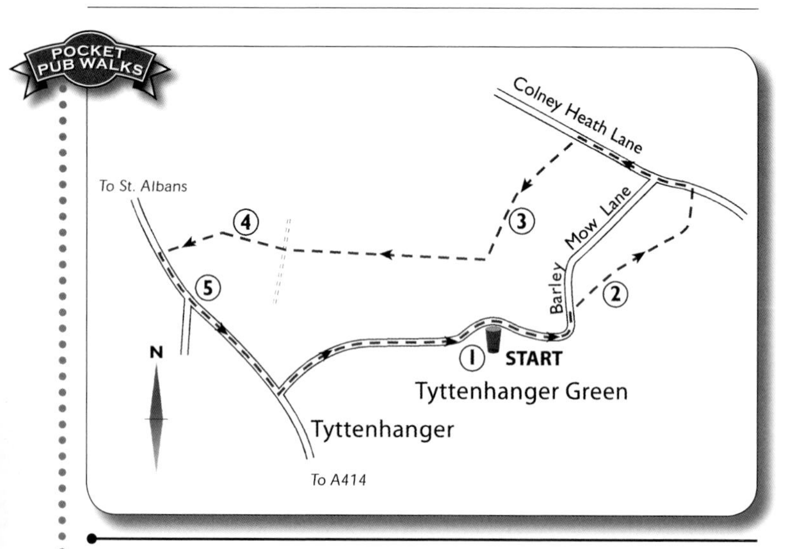

Open Monday to Friday from 11.30 am to 2.30 pm (3 pm on Saturday; and on Sunday from noon to 3 pm and 7 pm to 10.30 pm. Food is served from noon to 2 pm, seven days a week.
☎ 01727 857777

1 Turn right out of the pub and follow **Barley Mow Lane,** passing the footpaths on either side of you. After roughly ½ mile you come to a large white building where it's possible to make out an old pub sign: that of the Barley Mow. At the bend in the road here pick up the footpath on the right by the entrance to the **Barley Mow Stables**. This is channelled between two fences and emerges at the back of the stables. Keep going forward, through a wooden kissing gate, and across a small bridge over a dry stream.

2 Go straight across the field, aiming for the top right-hand corner. On reaching a small clearing, aim for the hedge in front of you, crossing through a gap to the other side so that it is on your left. Follow the hedge line until it runs out, at which point you need to head half left, aiming for a stile in the hedge by the side of a road, **Colney Heath Lane**. Cross the stile into the road and turn left. Pass the end of **Barley Mow Lane** and just before the speed limit sign follow the fingerpost on your left for **footpath 33**, to **Tyttenhanger**.

3 Pass along the left-hand edge of a large field and, about two thirds of the way up, turn right through a gap in the hedge and resume your direction, but with the hedge now on your right. A short way before the path becomes a concrete track, pick up the track passing to your right alongside a hedge and heading due

The striking Verulamium Museum on the outskirts of the city of St Albans.

east. This crosses a track known as **Hixberry Lane**, well loved by cyclists, where you need to turn right and then immediately left into a new field. Keep to the path as it passes through a gap shortly afterwards and into a cultivated field on the left.

4 Follow the edge of this field as it goes straight on and then to the left — some football pitches become visible through the hedge to the right — eventually dipping down to the right, through some trees, and emerging onto one of the pitches. Keep straight ahead until you reach a road by the bottom left-hand corner. Turn left and follow the roadside.

5 You now enter an area of relatively recent residential development, with a derelict farm to the left. (It's difficult to imagine now but until recently this was the site of one of a series of mental health institutions scattered across the north-west of London, this one being known as Cell Barnes Hospital.) On reaching a bend in the road, turn left into **Highfield Lane**, signed to **Tyttenhanger**. Follow this past some houses and take the first road on the left, **Tyttenhanger Green**. This meanders back to the pub, along the way passing an unusual white house clad almost entirely in corrugated iron.

Places of interest nearby

The award-winning **Verulamium Museum**, to the west of St Albans, sits on the edge of a large park with two lakes, one of which is popular with model boat enthusiasts. In the museum itself there are recreated Roman rooms and hands-on discovery areas, and some excellent mosaics. In the park there is also a Roman hypocaust, a mosaic-tiled heated floor, which has recently received a makeover.
☎ *01727 751810*

8 Ickleford

The Plume of Feathers

Separated from Hitchin by the River Oughton, Ickleford retains a strong sense of community and is clustered around a large green. The walk takes in part of the village but strikes out to the west to take advantage of the open fields and delights of Oughtonhead Common, a local wildlife reserve which traces the river from its first appearance and provides a selection of perfect picnic spots along the way. Wildlife is also a feature of one of the roadside verges along the route which has been designated a protected area by the local wildlife trust. There is some riverside strolling and the opportunity to take advantage of long views stretching out across Bedfordshire, making this a walk to take slowly rather than rush.

THE PUB

Sited just off the High Street, the **Plume of Feathers** is a friendly pub run by two sisters. There is a large, beamed, L-shaped bar and a separate dining area, as well as a secluded garden. As a 'real ale' pub, it offers a choice of beers, including Young's Bitter and Wadworth 6X, as well as guest beers. The pub hosts an annual beer festival in May. Fish is a feature of the menu here, with dishes such as halibut with red pepper butter, although there's also a selection of home-made pies with various fillings. Desserts are a highlight, with brandy snap and Belgian chocolate basket a favourite and one way of replacing the calories lost during the walk!

Open Monday to Thursday from 11 am to 3 pm and from 6 pm to 11 pm, all day Friday and Saturday (11 am to 11 pm), and from 11 am to 10.30 pm on Sunday
☎ *01462 432729*

1 Turn left out of the pub and follow the road as it curves to the left past the sports and recreation ground; soon after, pick up

Distance 5½ miles

Terrain Easy, with one or two slight gradients, and near the river just one steep bank to negotiate

OS Explorer 193 Luton and Stevenage, GR182317

Starting point The pub in Upper Green, off the High Street; use the large car park with permission. There is also limited public parking by the churchyard near the Old George pub.

How to get there *Ickleford lies 400 yards to the east of the A600, a mile north of Hitchin.*

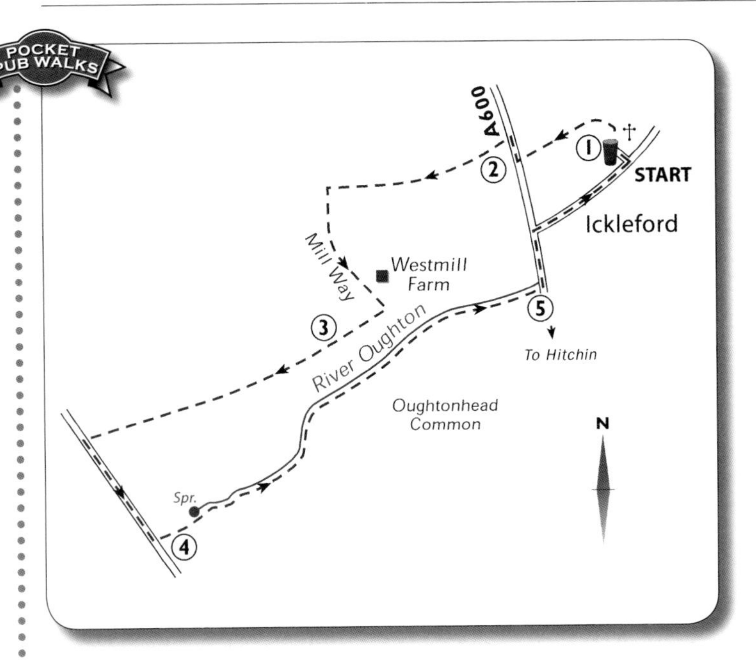

footpath 15, signed to **Pirton**. This is a firm, wide track, passing open fields to the right. At a road, with some disused greenhouses on the left, cross over and turn right, using the new path guarded by a wooden rail.

2 After about 100 yards, pick up the public bridleway on your left to cut through a couple of vast cultivated fields, with wide-ranging views towards the neighbouring county of **Bedfordshire**. Keep heading due west, ignoring a path on your left and eventually following a hedge, also on your left. After 100 yards or so, take the bridleway (signed to **Hitchin** and known as **Mill Way**) to your left and head south to **Westmill Lane**. (There is a seat along the way, should you feel the need to rest.) Turn right here, passing through a dilapidated metal gate and ignoring the path in front of you.

A delightful picnic spot beside the River Oughton near Ickleford.

3 The path runs slightly downhill and is marked with three clear ruts — two made by vehicles and one by walkers and riders — and offers great views over the surrounding countryside. After a short and gentle climb, the path snakes its way up to a junction with a country lane, where you turn left. Pause here to take in the view and then proceed along the verge, taking care, as it can get busy here. However, by way of compensation, this is a designated wildlife site, under the care of the Hertfordshire and Middlesex Wildlife Trust.

4 After a few hundred yards you come to a pumping station on your left and shortly after a 'road used as a footpath', which you follow. The pumping station marks the source of the **River Oughton**, your companion for most of the rest of the walk. Follow the path until it swings to the right; here your route is straight on, down a steep bank, at the base of which the river makes its first appearance. The path now follows a pleasant wooded glade with mature trees, many of which have fallen and present occasional obstacles on your way. There are one or two clearings along here which make good picnic spots, although generally the path sticks doggedly to the side of the river, with the odd temporary diversion. Ignore the footbridge to your right and continue in an eastward direction, passing a small weir on the way.

5 On reaching a large willow, the path leads onto a road, which you cross, and then head left along the pavement. Just after the sign for **Ickleford**, turn right at the roundabout and follow the path into the heart of the village. Look out here for the rather grand bus shelter, donated in 1935 by the local lord of the manor to commemorate the Silver Jubilee of George V. The village pump (which sits at the junction with **Upper Green**, where you are within sight of your starting point) was restored in 2002. It is over 100 years old and was manufactured by the Coalbrookdale Company, which was also responsible for the first iron bridge.

Places of interest nearby

Nearby, Letchworth is of interest as the country's first 'garden city', a fact recorded in the **First Garden City Heritage Museum**. The museum, sited in a unique building celebrating Letchworth's centenary in 2007, tracks the history of the garden city movement as inspired by the pioneer Ebenezer Howard, and the realization of this vision in Letchworth.

☎ *01462 482710*

9 Whitwell

The Maidens Head

Whitwell remains gloriously untouched by time, with old cottages along its main street. A watercress farm can be found at Nine Wells, to the west of the village, where bunches of this nutritious 'superfood' can be bought from the farm shop. Watercress is a sign of pure water, and this is confirmed by the clarity of the River Mimram, which is crossed twice on this walk.

The route begins by passing through horse pasture and then takes a circular path around the grounds of St Paul's Walden, the birthplace and childhood home of the late Queen Elizabeth, The Queen Mother, following parts of the Hertfordshire Way in its early stages. Passing All Saints' church, it then heads into bluebell-rich woodland, and offers a lot of variety in a relatively short distance before re-emerging in the village.

THE PUB

A two bar pub, the **Maidens Head** sits in the centre of the High Street and is known for its friendly welcome. It is a regular winner of the 'North Hertfordshire Pub of the Year', and was also recently awarded the accolade of 'Anglian Pub of the Year'. There's a cabinet of old Dinky cars by the public bar and various pictures and awards elsewhere on the walls. A flagship pub for local brewers McMullen, who have owned the place for over a century, the pub serves their own AK and Country, as well as guest beers. There is an extensive menu, which includes pollo (chicken pieces in a cream, mushroom, pepper and garlic sauce), which the menu claims is 'serviced with rice', as well as a range of double-decker sandwiches and the usual array of baguettes and burgers.

Open Monday to Saturday from 11 am to 3 pm and from 5 pm to 11 pm; and on Sunday from 7 pm to 11.30 pm. Food is served at lunchtime.
☎ *01483 871392*

Distance 2½ miles

OS Explorer 193 Luton and Stevenage, GR 184212

Terrain Some slight hills and a combination of field and woodland walking mostly along solid paths

Starting point The pub in the High Street; there's parking (with landlord's permission) in the car park over the road and also on the street.

How to get there *Whitwell lies on the B651, 2 miles north of Kimpton and 4 miles west of Stevenage.*

St Paul's Walden Bury, the childhood home of the late Queen Elizabeth, The Queen Mother.

1 Turn right out of the pub and walk up the **High Street**. Take care to look at some of the houses along the way, whose names yield up clues to the village's past life. At **Mill House** follow the signs to the left for the **Chiltern Way** extension (to the **Hertfordshire Way**), passing to the left of the buildings in front of you, which have an old grindstone propped against them. Cross over a stile, go through some grazing, and cross the **River Mimram** by the concrete bridge, which precedes another stile. Cross this, and shortly after a road; then go over another stile in front of you.

2 Continue slightly uphill, past a dead tree silhouetted against the skyline. (At the top of the hill pause for a moment to turn round and enjoy the view you've just earned, which shows off the valley carved by the Mimram, in which Whitwell nestles.) Stay on the path as it passes to the right of further grazing beyond a rather splendid oak tree and through various gates, bringing you to a road which leads to **St Paul's Walden Bury**. This was the birthplace and childhood home of the late Queen Mother and is still owned by the Bowes Lyon family, who have lived here since 1725.

3 Turn right and follow the road, passing a magnificent avenue of trees to your right. If you look to your left, you'll see they form a vista from the house. On reaching a grass triangle, pass to the left and walk past an interesting house with a front door shaped like a bishop's mitre, a form echoed in the windows. The path now becomes more of a track, heading uphill. This leads to **All Saints' church** at **St Paul's Walden,** with its impressively neat churchyard. Turn left here and continue until you reach **The Lodge**, where you pick up the footpath on your left which passes between hedges separating two fields.

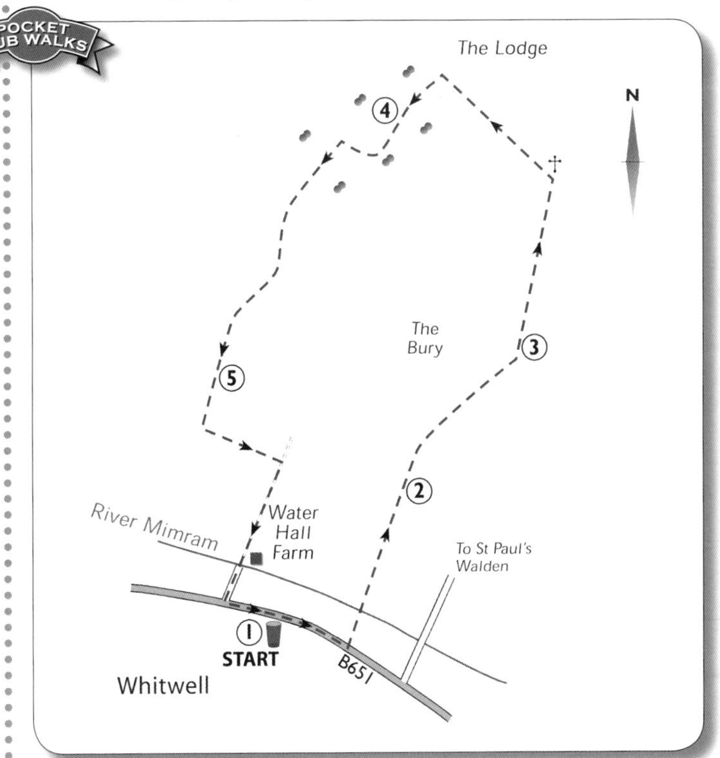

4 You now enter woodland, with low hanging branches which may take taller walkers by surprise. (A good spot for bluebells in late spring, the wood on your left is known, appropriately enough, as **Walk Wood**.) Pools of water and small brooks appear; the otherwise calm silence is broken only by the sounds of local wildlife. The path eventually emerges from the woods into an unused field.

5 Follow the right-hand boundary of this field, passing through a series of wooden kissing gates, with **Whitwell** now visible below although still a little way off. Continue along the path as it turns 90 degrees to the left, following an electric fence. After about 200 yards, the path slopes lazily down to the right and passes through a gate onto a track. Turn left here and then, shortly afterwards, right, heading steadily downhill. On crossing the river again you come to **Water Hall Farm** (see Places of interest below) on your left and some impressive wisteria-clad cottages. At the road head left, passing the post office, to return to your starting point.

Places of interest nearby

Water Hall Farm and Craft Centre in the village has rare breeds and a children's play area as well as the Higgletea Piggletea tearoom and gardens. It is open at the weekend and daily during school holidays.
☎ *01438 871256*

Slightly further afield, **Knebworth House**, between Whitwell and Stevenage, is a Gothic mansion owned by the Lytton family since 1490. The house and gardens can be viewed, and there is an adventure playground for children.
☎ *01438 812661*

10 Tewin

The Rose & Crown

In a haven of quiet outside Welwyn, this short stroll offers a good way to walk off a good lunch — or to establish an appetite for one! Tewin itself is a fairly ancient village and can trace its history back to Saxon times. The centre of the village is dominated by a charming and large triangular green, which is where you find the pub. Look out also for the Old School House on Lower Green, which some claim was a model for Dotheboys Hall in Dickens' *Nicholas Nickleby*.

Distance 3½ miles

OS Explorer 182 St Albans and Hatfield, GR 272148

Terrain Mainly on solid tracks with some short hill climbs

Starting point The pub on Lower Green; there is parking (with landlord's permission) in the car park; also on the street.

How to get there *Tewin sits a mile north of the B1000, north-east of Welwyn.*

The walk is mainly along solid tracks and starts behind the pub, adjacent to a good blackberry spot; so bring some bags or pots if it's the right time of year. It then passes through some woods and emerges onto open fields where there's an excellent view of the Digswell viaduct. Completed in 1850 for the Great Northern Railway, this was deliberately designed to mimic a Roman aqueduct, something it achieves with distinction, and was built in only two years. The second half of the walk is along the valley of the River Mimram, although the water is sadly not visible, and arcs round the back of the village by the local bowls club.

THE PUB

Impossible to miss, the **Rose & Crown**, on the edge of Lower Green, has two bars. The one leading from the car park is decorated on the beams of the low ceiling with literary quotations. The wood that dominates the floor and walls creates a certain amount of echo in the pub, but if you want some peace and quiet there's a sun trap patio just outside. Thirsts can be quenched with Greene King IPA and Abbot Ale, and there's also a wine list to complement the pub's seafood specialities, which include delicacies such as grilled sardines in chilli salsa, fresh calamari and Cromer crab. There is also a 'Lite

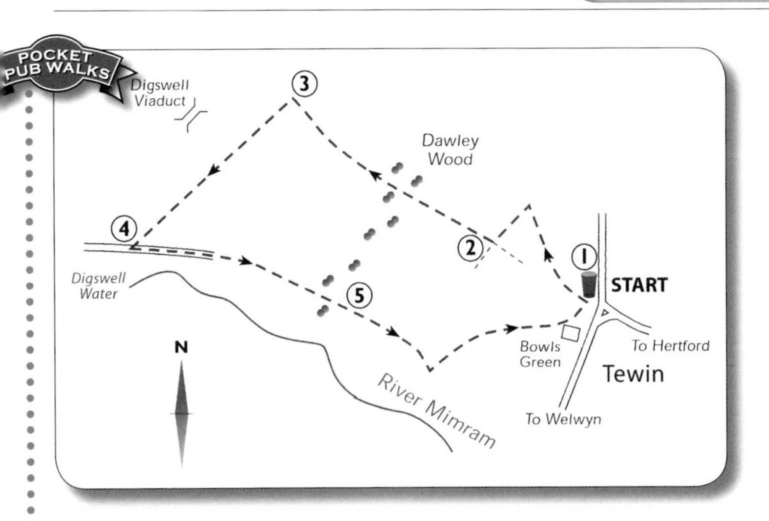

Bites' menu, the highlight of which is probably the seasonal vegetable Spanish omelette.

Open Monday to Friday from noon to 3 pm and from 6 pm to 11 pm and at the weekend from 11 am, closing at 11 pm on Saturday and at 10.30 pm on Sunday. Food is served from noon to 2 pm, Monday to Saturday, and from 7 pm to 9 pm, Tuesday to Saturday; and from 12.30 pm to 3.30 pm on Sunday, when the speciality is a roast.
☎ *01483 717257*

1 Turn left out of the pub and immediately walk down **Back Lane**, which is marked as a public byway, and soon narrows down to a small track lined with brambles. After the entrance to a farm and a small pond, the track goes to the left, marked with a red arrow, and the view opens up, with woodlands to the right and **Welwyn** to the left. At a T-junction, which is in fact a crossing of paths, bear right, following the blue arrow and heading for the woodland, known as **Dawley Wood**.

2 The path now heads straight for the trees, climbing a hill as it does so. The woods on either side are used for sports such as orienteering. There follows a fairly sharp downhill section, which eventually comes out onto open fields. Continue along the path, which then narrows down and climbs gently uphill. Ignore the first path to your left, and shortly after the path widens out again and comes out behind some houses, very briefly becoming a metalled road.

3 Almost immediately the path heads left, down a bridleway signed to **Digswell**. On emerging from the trees, there is a choice

An impressive view of the Digswell viaduct.

of paths across a field; take the one on your right, which heads slightly downhill, taking a wide corner off the field. You are now going in a south-westerly direction, straight towards **Digswell viaduct**. (This impressive feature carries the East Coast main line. With only two tracks, it is something of a bottleneck on the line and is therefore always fairly busy with traffic.)

4 When you reach a road, turn immediately left, along the bottom of the field you've just crossed, following signs to **Tewin**. (You are now following the line of the River Mimram, but sadly it is not visible from here and even the field is slightly raised above you.) After a hundred yards or so, maintain your direction at the junction with another path, by a wooden kissing gate, and follow the path as it heads downhill and then uphill and into some trees.

5 Follow the path as it peaks again in the woods and emerges on the other side. About 150 yards before some more woods, there is a clear diversion, marked with a yellow arrow, going to the left of a partially hidden house, which you need to take. At a T-junction head right and then immediately left, and on reaching a Y-junction go left and down a hedge-lined alley by the immaculately kept bowling green. This brings you to a wooden kissing gate, the back of the pub, and your starting point.

Places of interest nearby

Slightly out of town, at the junction of the A1(M) and B1000, sits the **Welwyn Roman Bathhouse**, the remains of a bathhouse which was attached to a Roman villa. The series of hot and cold rooms and hypocaust, built 1,700 years ago, sit together in a vault under the A1. The baths are open from 2 pm to 5 pm during school holidays, at the weekends, and on bank holidays.
☎ *01707 271362*

11 Walkern

The White Lion

Walkern has a somewhat spooky past. Legend has it that its site was chosen by none other than the Devil, who moved building stones intended for a church at nearby Boxbury, intoning 'Walk on, walk on!' as he did so, thus giving the village its name. Whether you believe this or not, it is fact that it was the home of Jane Wenham, one of the country's last convicted witches (some say the last). It was believed that witches were unable to say the Lord's Prayer, so when she stumbled while reciting the prayer at her trial in 1712, her conviction was secured. She was later given a Queen's Pardon, however, and lived elsewhere until her death in 1730.

These days things are more subdued, which may be due in part to the three pubs that this small and surprising village manages to support. Another feature is the local community shop, a sign that the village is more than a mere commuter haunt perhaps? The walk takes in the north-western side of the surrounding land and passes amongst a number of springs, allowing the walker to enjoy both views and some pleasant and not too strenuous rural strolling, and there are plenty of blackberrying opportunities amongst the mature hedgerows in late summer.

THE PUB

The northernmost of a run of three pubs, the **White Lion** dates from the 16th century and has lots of nooks and crannies, including a corner with games, a small TV, and a sofa by a fire, a scene which could be lifted from someone's front room. The walls are decorated with old advertising boards and photographs of past events in the pub. There's a large garden and a separate restaurant, although the bar menu is more than adequate. Dishes include home-made soup, steak and ale pie, and even a 'design your own' omelette, as well as sausage and mash in Yorkshire pudding. Beers include Greene King and Old Speckled Hen, and there is also a selection of wine.

Distance 3½ miles

OS Explorer 193 Luton and Stevenage, GR 289265

Terrain One or two slight gradients; the going is pretty firm, although parts may get muddy in winter

Starting point The pub; parking (with landlord's permission) in the pub car park

How to get there *Walkern sits just east of Stevenage on the B1037.*

Open Monday to Thursday from noon to 2.30 pm and from 4 pm to 11 pm; from noon to midnight on Friday and Saturday; and from noon to 10.30 pm on Sunday. Food is served from noon to 2.30 pm, Monday to Friday (noon to 3 pm on Saturday), and from 6 pm to 9.30 pm, Tuesday to Saturday; and from noon to 5 pm on Sunday.
☎ *01438 861251*

1 Turn right out of the pub and then left down the track on the other side of the road, signed to **Warren Green**. (This is by an unusual octagonal building by a pond in the grounds of **Manor Farm** and is known as **Dovehouse Lane**.) The track runs alongside the farm buildings before heading up the left-hand edge of a large field and continuing past a fingerpost indicating another path. Follow the track as it goes gently uphill, passing

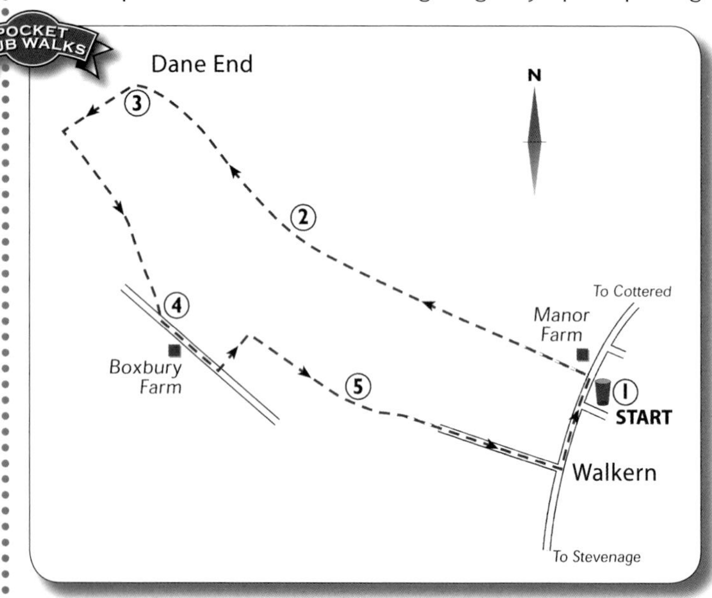

The octagonal building at Walkern near the start of the walk.

another path, this time to the left, and, eventually, a third, to the right.

2 The track is lined by occasional mature oaks and in places it can be churned up at times owing to tractor activity. There are three springs in the valley to the left but their locations are hard to make out. Keep to the left-hand edge of the field as the track finally diverges to the right, keeping a small copse of trees to your left. At the far end of the copse, the path emerges onto a smaller field and heads down towards **Dane End**.

3 In front of a farmhouse is a three-way junction of paths; you need to take the one going left, marked with a blue arrow to signify its

status as a bridleway. This takes you slightly downhill, with some vivid red-tiled houses in the distance in front of you. At a clearing by a telegraph pole, take the path to the left (marked with a yellow arrow), passing a notice telling you that Thames Water maintain the local springs. The path is quite narrow at first but opens out after a short while, alongside some mature blackthorn bushes on the right.

4 At the four black grain silos at **Boxbury Farm**, the path diverts to the left and quickly becomes a road, which you follow for 200 yards or so before picking up the footpath to the left, just after a solitary oak. (This does require a short scramble up a bank.) Follow the path across the field, climbing steadily uphill, at 90 degrees to the road. Shortly after it flattens out, the path meets a junction, where you turn right, just beyond the field boundary. This now takes you slightly downhill.

5 At the corner of the field there is a choice of paths and you need to keep straight on, down a track bounded by hedges. This eventually widens out and becomes the more formal residential road known as **Froghall Lane**, which you follow onto the **High Street**. Turn left here, opposite the shop, and continue along it, noting the community shop on the right, as well as the other two pubs, the **Robin Hood** and the **Yew Tree**. After 200 yards or so you will come to your starting point.

Places of interest nearby

Benington Lordship, south-east of Walkern, is a spectacular garden which is occasionally open to the public (check beforehand). As well as a rose garden and herbaceous borders, there is an extensive kitchen garden, a rockery, a large pond, and even a Norman keep next to the more modern house.

☎ *08701 261709*

12 Newgate Street

The Coach & Horses

This is a straightforward walk, broadly following a square around the grounds of Ponsbourne Park, which was once owned by Sir Thomas Seymour, who married Catherine Parr after she became Henry VIII's widow. The modern house is less ancient, however. The grounds are well kept, and complete this walk, the first half of which is on part of the Hertfordshire Chain Walk. This innovative idea, created by the East Hertfordshire

Distance 2½ miles

OS Explorer 182 St Albans and Hatfield and 174 Epping Forest and Lee Valley. GR 303050

Terrain Mainly bridleways and paths, with a section through woods and one or two small hills, but nothing serious

Starting point The pub, where there is also parking (with landlord's permission).

How to get there *Newgate Street is 2 miles east of Brookman's Park, on a minor road off the B158.*

Footpath Society, involves fifteen linked circular walks through the villages in the east of the county.

Part of the latter section includes a stroll through The Warren, a small wood noted for its rhododendrons, after which the route rises to Tylers Causeway. Newgate Street is a medium sized village with two pubs and an attractive church. If you have time, go about a mile east of the village to the railway bridge to spot one of Hertfordshire's coal posts. These metal posts bearing the arms of the City of London were erected after the Coal Duties Act of 1851 and acted as tax points; there were 250 of them dotted around the capital's perimeter. The funds thus raised were subsequently used to build many of London's bridges.

THE PUB

A split-level pub with a large beer garden and a children's play area at the back, the **Coach & Horses** occupies a road-front setting in the heart of the village, next to the church, and is particularly popular with families on warm summer evenings. A solid rustic feel combines with more modern accoutrements such as a large flat screen TV and slot machine, although these are hidden away on one of the levels. There's no shortage of seating, both inside and out, where you can enjoy a pint of Black Sheep, Adnams, or Greene King IPA. The lunchtime speciality is a range of toasted ciabatta sandwiches served with corn chips. Favourites include a Mediterranean vegetable melt and a vegetarian sausage with caramelized onions. There is also a range of ploughman's and baked potatoes as well as more substantial meals.

Open Monday to Saturday from 11 am to 11 pm, and from 11 am to 11.30 pm on Sunday. Food is served throughout except on Sunday evening.
☎ *01707 872326*

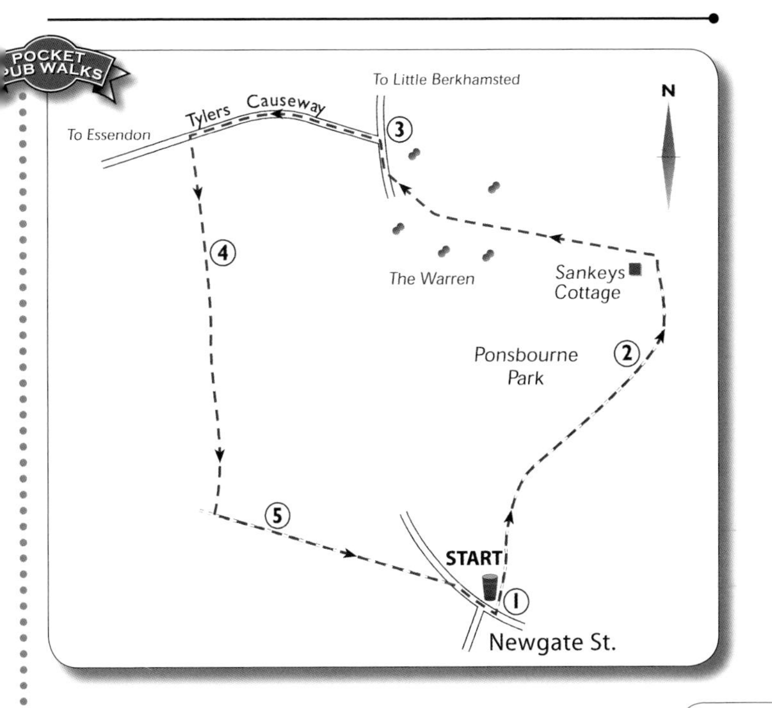

Ponsbourne Park was once owned by Sir Thomas Seymour.

1 Turn left out of the pub and on the left by a white painted house go down the track leading to the **Ponsbourne Park Hotel** and marked as a public bridleway. This part of the walk follows the **Hertfordshire Chain Walk**. Ahead of you the hotel appears from amongst the trees, its golf course visible on the left. The route now goes downhill and then a little steeply uphill, but it's nothing too difficult and is soon dispensed with.

2 Keep on the track past the front of the hotel and up to Home Farm, where the path becomes less solid and forks to the left before heading up a slight hill. A large and rather impressive wall hiding a tennis court occupies the view to the left, shortly after which, by **Sankeys Cottage**, the path heads sharp left down a public bridleway, which leads almost immediately into some trees known as **The Warren**. True to the name, the path now twists and turns through the trees, although it is firm throughout and easy walking. This is a particularly pretty part of the walk in early summer when there is a profusion of light pink and purple rhododendrons on both sides of the track.

3 On reaching a road by a newly built house, cross over onto **Tyler's Causeway**, signed to **Essendon**. Stay on this road past an elegant black and white shuttered house until you reach **Ivy Cottage Kennels** on your right. Opposite is a fresh public footpath by a house called **Foxwood**, although the sign is slightly hidden. Take this, following the left-hand edge of a meadow, the first point at which you go 'off-road' on this particular walk.

4 On a straight, southward trajectory you pass further meadows and then less productive fields, eventually coming out on the other side of the golf course seen earlier; there is a small muddy pond on the right. The route now climbs a hill and comes to the corner of a field, to continue just ahead of you. However, the path is not immediately obvious and it is unmarked. Happily, this is only a temporary aberration, as it soon opens out onto a small paddock, at the end of which it reaches a minor road, where you turn left.

5 Continue along the road, which acquires a pavement as you wander past modern detached houses and then older semi-detached properties, finishing by a children's playground and the local church, dedicated to St Mary. Cross the road in front of you and bear right, soon to arrive back at the **Coach & Horses** and your starting point.

Places of interest nearby

Capel Manor Gardens near Cuffley offer a colourful oasis around a Georgian manor house and Victorian stables. There are over 30 themed gardens, including an Italianate maze and a Japanese garden — not surprising really, as this is home to a specialist college of horticulture. There are also animals, including heavy horses, and shows throughout the year.

☎ *08456 122122*

13 Cottered

The Bull

Despite being on a fairly busy A-road, Cottered has retained its distinctive charm, with a number of thatched cottages and other buildings of architectural merit. The church, which often provides a beacon along the walk, is worth a visit for its large 15th century painting of St Christopher, to whom the church is dedicated. It depicts the saint carrying the Christ child, and is remarkable as much for the detail of its background as its central figures.

Distance 3½ miles

OS Explorer 194 Hertford and Bishop's Stortford, GR 321294

Terrain Mainly flat, apart from one or two short but gentle hills

Starting point The pub; parking in the pub car park (with landlord's permission).

How to get there *Cottered is on the A507, 2 miles west of Buntingford.*

A number of footpaths converge on the village and this walk takes advantage of some of them to give a sense of its position in the surrounding countryside, and there are plenty of mature hedgerows along the way, marking out ancient field boundaries. Utilizing bridleways and field paths, the walk is an easy and steady one, that is suitable for all ages and provides the perfect way to build up an appetite for one of the pub's generous platters.

THE PUB

Opposite a row of pretty thatched cottages, the **Bull** in Cottered is an airy welcoming pub with a long narrow bar and a restaurant. Recently extended and refurbished, the interior neatly combines a modern feel with a traditional look. The menu (which earned the pub a Specialist Food Operator of the Year award), carries the usual staples, including home-made burgers, along with an extensive range of more interesting dishes such as their omelette Arnold Bennett (made with smoked haddock and topped with béchamel sauce) and the 'blue plate', a daily fish special. Look out also for the impressive cheese trolley, perfect with a pint of Greene King.

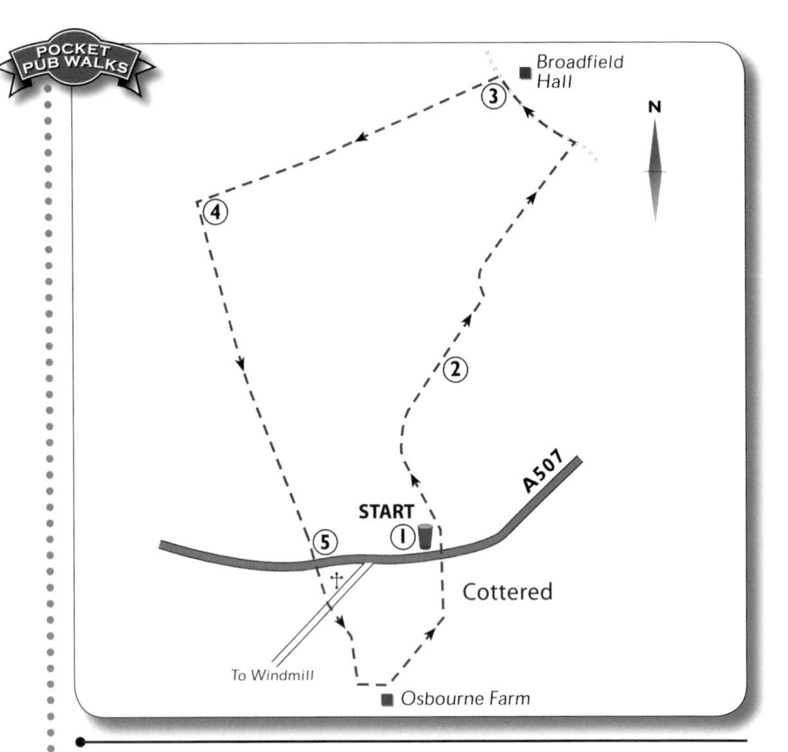

Open Monday to Saturday from noon to 2.30 pm (3 pm on Saturday) and from 6.30 pm to 11 pm; from noon to 3 pm and from 7 pm to 10.30 pm on Sunday. Food is served throughout the week from noon to 2 pm and from 6.30 pm (7 pm on Sunday) to 9.30 pm.

☎ *0 1763 281243*

1 Turn left out of the pub and go up the bridleway at the top of **Bull Lane** beside the pub, signed to Broadfield Hall. This bends to the right, then to the left, as it follows the edge of a field. This

is part of the **Hertfordshire Chain Walk** (see Walk 12) linking the east of the county with Cambridgeshire. Note the spire of the church to your left, which you will see again later. On reaching an open field, follow the path as it bears right, cutting across the corner of the field. At the far corner cut through a gap in the hedge and turn left, following the edge of the field.

2 Keep to the edge as it bends to the right and aim for the top corner, where a wooden platform takes you through another hedge. Now follow the bridleway, marked with a blue arrow, to the right. (The path is lined with a basic staked fence to the right and mature hedges to the left, resplendent with hawthorn berries, wild apples, blackberries and sloes.) At the road, turn left, heading gently downhill and bending slowly to the right before coming out onto an open space lined with newly planted trees on the right. Just before a sharp bend to the right, take the path to the left marked 'road used as a path'. (The road goes on to **Broadfield Hall**, an elegant private house.)

3 As the sign might suggest, this is a rough track, cutting across a field. At the side of a small linear copse look out in summer for sectioned-off areas used for growing maize and sunflowers. Passing a path to the left, keep your direction on the path marked with rather ominous black arrows, to emerge

Some attractive thatched cottages in Cottered.

onto open fields and a gentle downward slope. At the end of the field, bear right, pass through a gap, and go up along the side of another field. Follow a blue arrow left, keeping the hedge to your right.

4 Soon afterwards, pick up the footpath on the left which cuts across the field. Go to the right of the pylon in the corner and over a ditch which carries a feeder to the **River Beane.** Head now for the church spire seen earlier in the walk. The path starts on a grassy bank but soon becomes a cutting, where there is some evidence of badger sets. It then emerges from the cutting at the peak of the climb and begins to fall, becoming more of a track as it does so.

5 When you reach the road, cross over and pass the front of the church. Cross over the next junction also and go down **Warren Lane**, past the weather-boarded barns of **Cheynes Farm**. At **Osbourne Farm**, turn left and follow the slightly overgrown path over a stile and then over two more. Now pick up the footpath on your left and head half right over a field and over another stile. Then aim for a point halfway along the left-hand border of the field and pass through a kissing gate. Go through another gate to your right and head immediately left, down the side of a playground and cricket pavilion. Go down a gap in the hedge to emerge in front of the pub.

Places of interest nearby

Cromer Windmill, a mile to the west of Cottered, is the last remaining postmill in Hertfordshire. It dates back to 1679 and was restored during the latter part of the last century. Visits are possible from the second Sunday in May until mid-September on Sundays and Bank Holidays and on the second and fourth Saturdays each month.
☎ *01279 843301*

14 Chapmore End

The Woodman

This part of the county harbours all sorts of secrets, many of them underground. Not only are there dark tales of secret passageways linking Bengeo Temple Farm all the way to Hertford, but Ware to the south also holds its own subterranean mysteries (see Places of Interest Nearby).

This walk links the charming hamlet of Chapmore End, distinctive for its large village pond, with Wadesmill and the River Rib. The route follows either side of the valley created by the river and affords some good views, although the water is strangely reluctant to make an appearance. The going is relatively easy, across mainly open land with occasional woodland offering variety, and includes one or two fairly challenging climbs, but nothing too daunting.

THE PUB Sitting next to the pond at the heart of the village, the **Woodman** is a snug local; its two bars have wooden floors and wainscots, and neither is capable of taking a crowd. The large garden more than makes up for this, however, as does the warm welcome and inviting sight of beer drawn straight from the barrel behind the bar. Ales on offer in this Greene King pub include Abbot and IPA, as well as a range of guest beers. The temptation to linger is reinforced by a well-stocked bookcase on one wall and a piano against another. Lunchtime snacks are served daily (except Monday), with generous sandwiches (including roast topside of beef) and ploughman's, as well as a cheeseboard for two. Gourmet meals are served on Thursday evenings and can include such delights as braised lamb shank or roast monkfish with parma ham.

Distance 5½ miles

OS Explorer 194 Hertford and Bishop's Stortford, GR 328164

Terrain Mainly across fields with a few steep climbs

Starting point The pub by the pond; park either by the pond or in the pub car park (with the landlord's permission).

How to get there *Chapmore End lies just north of the B158, 2 miles west of Wadesmill, itself on the A10, 2 miles north of Ware.*

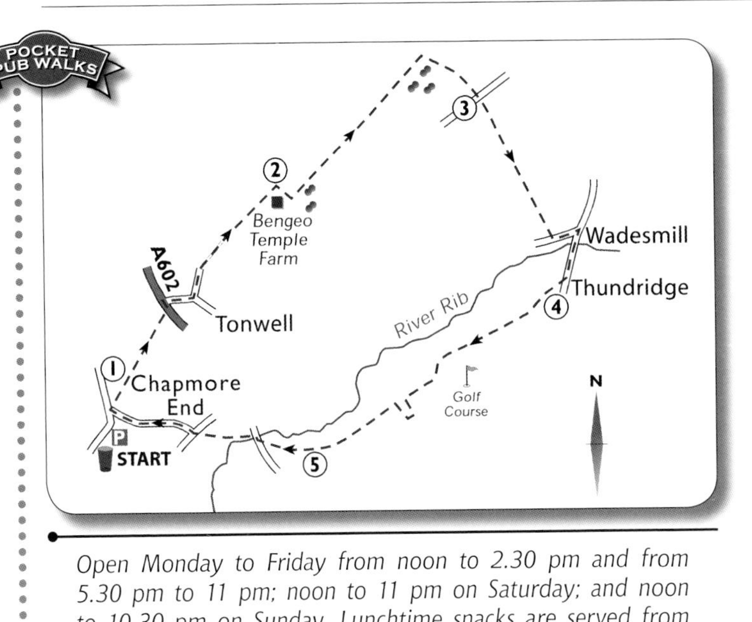

Open Monday to Friday from noon to 2.30 pm and from 5.30 pm to 11 pm; noon to 11 pm on Saturday; and noon to 10.30 pm on Sunday. Lunchtime snacks are served from noon to 2 pm, Tuesday to Sunday.
☎ 01920 463143

1 Turn right out of the pub and pick up the footpath by the phone box at the top of the pond, signed to **Tonwell**. This takes you along the side of a field in the direction of a water tower shaped like an inverted pyramid. The path is firm and soon opens out to give good views to the right. Cross over a dry stream and on meeting the A602 cross over and go up **Ware Road**. Pass a pub on your right and turn left up **Temple Lane**, passing the water tower at the top. The lane dissolves into a track heading slightly uphill towards **Bengeo Temple Farm**. (This farm was recently in the news when it was revealed as the destination of secret underground tunnels said to have been dug by the Knights Templar.)

2 Follow the waymark to the left of the farm and after negotiating a kissing gate bear right to go round the back of the farm. After passing through another kissing gate, turn left and follow a track downhill into some woods. At a Y-junction shortly after entering the wood, take the left-hand option, which soon emerges into open fields. Follow the path for ½ mile until you reach some woods; at the top turn right, or south-east, following the woodland edge.

3 Keep ahead at the next junction and cut straight across a large open field before passing briefly through trees and across another field. You now start to plunge downhill into **Wadesmill**. (Wadesmill's claim to fame is as the place where slave campaigner Thomas Clarkson is said have experienced his conversion to his life's cause following a revelation from God.) On reaching the road, turn left and go into the heart of Wadesmill. By the **Anchor** pub, turn right and soon cross the **River Rib**. On the far side of the bridge is **Thundridge**, although, perversely perhaps, this is the location of **Wadesmill Stores**.

4 Pick up the footpath on the right, just after the bus stop; here there are good views over the **Rib valley**. Initially this is a fairly solid track leading up to some allotments, but it soon narrows after the entrance to a sports field. Beyond a stile you come out onto a golf course. Maintain a generally south-westerly direction, making a detour to the left to bypass some disused gravel pits. The route then leads up to a track on the left-hand edge of the course. (Take care here; the path is close to some fairways and is poorly marked – look out for yellow tipped stakes.)

5 At the end of the golf course, the path widens out by **Westmill Cottage**. At the small side road, turn right, past an old mill building, and pick up the footpath on your left, signed to **Chapmore End**. Follow the path as it diverts to the right to allow you to pass under the road via a subway. Continue along the path on the other side of the subway as it heads left and then

right. You now walk briefly beside the **Rib** and along the side of a field to a small country lane, which you need to cross. Go up the road opposite, signed to the **Woodman**.

The village pond at Chapmore End.

Places of interest nearby

Continuing the theme of underground passageways, Ware is the home of **Scott's Grotto**, built by the Quaker poet John Scott in the 18th century. The country's largest grotto, it consists of six chambers linked by passageways and air tunnels and is lined with flints, fossils, and shells. Above ground it is crowned by an octagonal summerhouse. It is open only on Saturday afternoons and bank holidays between April and late September.
☎ *01920 464131*

15 Standon

The Star

Sited at the junction of the Roman Ermine Way and Stane Street, Standon enjoys an illustrious history. It has a 13th century church, founded by the Knights of St John, and many other historical buildings that make it worthwhile lingering after your walk, the route of which is undemanding physically but rewarding in terms of views and serendipity.

Unexpected finds include a well-preserved railway station without a line and a lump of Hertfordshire puddingstone, said to have magical properties. Amongst all this is the River Rib, a salmon river, said to be in the top ten per cent of such rivers in terms of the variety of invertebrate life it supports.

Distance 3½ miles

OS Explorer 194 Hertford and Bishop's Stortford, GR 396223

Terrain Relatively easy, on two well established paths with the occasional modest climb

Starting point The pub opposite the church; parking in the pub car park (with landlord's permission).

How to get there *Standon is a mile east of the A10, on the A120, 5 miles north of Ware.*

THE PUB

The **Star** in Standon is a little way off the High Street and benefits from its quieter location. Built in 1550, the pub is proud of its heritage, signs of which are clearly visible in the low oak beams that support the ceiling. There's a small bar, which is furnished more like someone's front room than a pub, and a large dining area. Here it is possible to sample a varied menu which offers dishes such as roasted vegetable Wellington, or mussel pot with shoestring fries. The highlight of the lunch menu is possibly the 'star porker', a Cumberland sausage in a baguette with fries. Outside there is a secluded garden, a large car park, and even a floodlit petanque court.

Open Monday to Friday from noon to 2.30 pm and from 5.30 pm to 11 pm; from noon to 11 pm on Saturday; and from noon to 10.30 pm on Sunday.
Food is served from noon to 2 pm and from 6.30 pm to 10.30 pm, Tuesday to Saturday; and from noon to 3 pm on Sunday.
☎ *01920 821258*

1 Turn left out of the pub and head back up the wide main street, passing the **Bell** on the way. Turn left at the T-junction and go over the **River Rib** before crossing the road using the pedestrian crossing; immediately in front of you is the impressive **Standon Flour Mill**. Walk up **Station Road** on your right and continue past some houses to a school. Go down the road leading into the school but before reaching the gates take the track on your right, following it into a field, where you bear left.

2 The route now takes you round the back of the school and takes on a decided straightness, explained by the fact that it follows

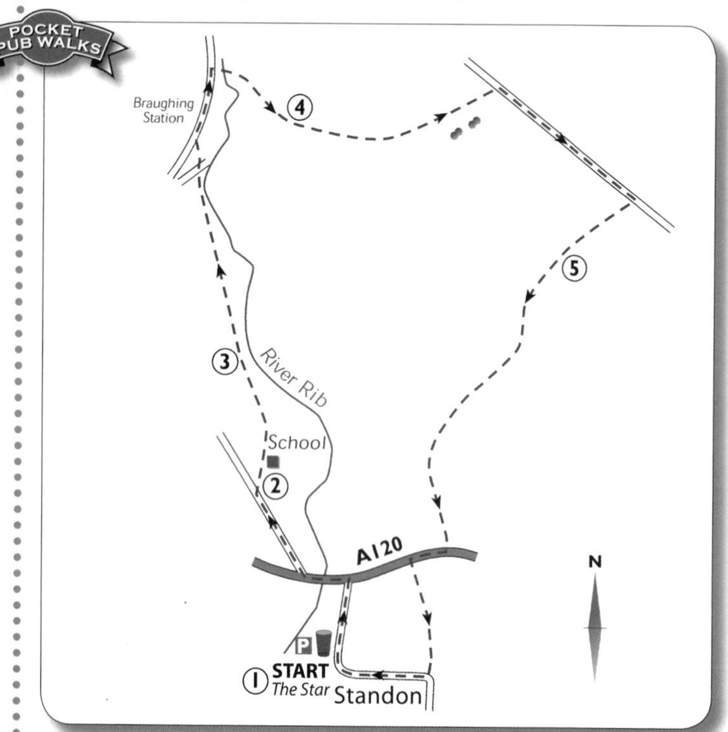

The well-preserved Braughing Station.

the path of a disused railway, once part of the Ware, Hadham and Buntingford Railway, which despite its name never actually went to Ware. The line of the railway becomes more apparent as you enter some trees and walk along the top of a cutting, the line lying in a dip below to the left. To add to the interest, the **River Rib** also comes alongside at this point.

3 The route now follows the side of a field and just before a road it becomes clear that the railway line was once on an embankment here. Go through a wooden kissing gate after a minor road. A solid square bridge looms into view as the path diverts to the right and on to another, larger, road. Be sure to look to the left, however, where **Braughing Station** (now a private residence) is clearly visible, including a carriage in a siding, a signal box, and other railway memorabilia. Continue to the right, crossing the river once again. In 100 yards pick up

the public bridleway on the other side of the road through a gate and up a track.

4 As the bridleway winds steadily uphill, there are great views over the **Rib Valley**. Emerging from the trees, the path goes to the right. At a junction of paths, go slightly beyond the blue waymarked sign and through some rhododendrons; then out onto an open field. Take care as this is not well marked. Aim for the north-eastern or top-left tip of the field, which brings you out onto a lane, where you turn right. At the brow of a short uphill section, pick up the public bridleway on your right, marked to **Standon**.

5 This is the **Harcamlow Way**, a figure of eight path taking in Harlow and Cambridge, hence its name. Pass the edge of a farmyard and on reaching a track bear left. At the road (the A120), follow the pavement on the right to enter the outskirts of **Standon**. Shortly after the speed sign, turn left up **Half Acres** and follow it as it draws you back into the countryside. On reaching another track, turn right and continue ahead on the road (**Hadham Road**) as it curves to the right past the **Standon Puddingstone**, reputed to be a charm against the 'evil eye'. Look out also for a well-preserved 16th century, timber-framed building. **Hadham Road** becomes **High Street** and brings you back to your starting point.

Places of interest nearby

The **Forge Museum** in Much Hadham is in a Grade II listed building which was the village forge for over 150 years under the proprietorship of a single family. It now houses an exhibition of the history of blacksmithing and farriery and has a resident working blacksmith. There is also a Victorian cottage garden here with a rare early 19th century bee shelter and a granary.

☎ *01279 843301*